THE GIFT FOR THE SEEKER
ITHAF AL-TALIB

Dar al-Arqam Educational Trust
16 Thurmaston Lane,
Leicester
LE5 0TE
United Kingdom

info@datrust.org
www.datrust.org

SECOND EDITION

By: al-Imām Abū Bakr b. Muḥammad Mullā al-Ḥanafī al-Aḥsā'ī
Translation: Mohammed Zaqir Shaikh
Cover Design & Typesetting: Imran Rahim ◆ Etherea Design
Cover art motif: Abdul Karim Mats Cederberg

ISBN 978-1-9998574-5-5

The Gift for the Seeker

Itḥāf al-Ṭālib

A Compendium of Compulsory Islamic Knowledge According to Orthodox Islam

al-Imām Abū Bakr b. Muḥammad
Mulla al-Ḥanafī al-Aḥsā'ī
(d. 1198 AH / 1784 CE)

Translation
Mohammed Zaqir Shaikh

بِسْمِ ٱللَّهِ ٱلرَّحْمَٰنِ ٱلرَّحِيمِ

Contents

بسم الله الرحمن الرحيم

الحمد لله المتصلة آلاؤه المتسلسلة نعماؤه والصلاة والسلام على نبي الرحمة والهدى وعلى آله وصحبه ومن بهم اقتدى أما بعد:

فإن الأخ في الله الشيخ: **ذاكر** أصلح الله حاله، وسدد أقواله وأفعاله، ممن شمر ساعده في طلب العلوم الشرعية، وجدَّ في تحصيله بالأمور المرعية، ورحل في سبيله وتغرَّب ولازم أهل العلم وانتفع بملازمتهم، ثم رجع إلى بلده بعد أن حصَّل من العلوم ما حصَّل واشتغل بتدريس العلوم الشرعية، وكان من بين المتون التي اشتغل بتدريسها متن "إتحاف الطالب" لجدي العلامة الشيخ أبوبكر الملا الحنفي الأحسائي المتوفى سنة (١٢٧٠هـ) وترجمه من اللغة العربية إلى اللغة الإنجليزية ليسهل تناوله عند أصحاب هذه اللغة فجزاه الله خيراً ونفع به.

وقد سألني الإجازة على هذا الكتاب النافع، فأقول وبالله التوفيق: قد أجزت الأخ المذكور، ضاعف الله لي وله الأجور على هذا الكتاب وعلى سائر مؤلفات الشيخ أبوبكر الملا، وأنا أرويها عن والدي الشيخ محمد والعم الشيخ عبدالرحمن عن والدهما الشيخ أبوبكر عن والده الشيخ عبدالله وهو يرويها عن مؤلفها الشيخ أبوبكر بن الشيخ محمد الملا آل الواعظ الحنفي الأحسائي، وأوصي أخي بالاستمرار في ميدان التعلم والتعليم، والدعوة إلى دين الله الحق المبين، بالحكمة والموعظة الحسنة، وأن لا ينساني من صالح دعواته.

وصلى الله وسلم وبارك على سيدنا محمد وعلى آله وصحبه وسلم.

وكتبه المفتقر إلى عفو المولى

يحيى بن الشيخ محمد بن أبي بكر الملا

عفا الله عنه

Authorisation

All praise be to Allah, He who is uninterrupted in conferring His blessings; continuous in bestowing His Grace. Salutations and peace be upon the messenger of mercy and guidance and upon his family, companions and those that follow him.

Indeed the brother in faith Shaykh Zaqir, Allah rectify his situation and guide his speech and actions, is from those that strived to attain sacred knowledge and endeavoured to imbue this with compiling sacred beneficial sciences. He travelled and became a stranger to the world, striving in the path of knowledge intensely associating with the people of knowledge and benefitting from their company. Returning to his homeland, after attaining licenses in various sciences he continued to impart sacred knowledge. From the sacred texts which he imparted was the didactic text 'The Gift for the Seeker' (*Ithaf al-Talib*) of my grandfather the erudite scholar Shaykh Abu Bakr al-Mulla al-Ahsai al-Hanafi (who passed on to the mercy of Allah in the year 1270 AH). The text was translated in to English to benefit English speakers, may Allah reward the translator and enable benefit to emanate from him.

I was requested to confer a license to teach this beneficial text. In response to this request; I pronounce, with Allah's Divine Grace; indeed I confer upon the aforementioned brother the licence to teach 'The Gift for the Seeker', may Allah multiply for him and me recompense via the means of this work and similarly all the works of Shaykh Abu Bakr al-Mulla. I narrate this text from my father Shaykh Mohammed and my uncle Shaykh Abd al-Rahman from their father Shaykh Abu Bakr from his father Shaykh Abd Allah who narrates it from the author Shaykh Abu Bakr son of Shaykh Mohammed al-Mulla al-Ahsai al-Hanafi. I entrust my brother to persevere within the field of sacred knowledge, imparting and learning it, exhorting with excellence to the manifest true religion of Allah with wisdom and to not forget me from the pious of your supplications. Allah's salutations, peace and blessings be upon our liege lord Mohammed and upon his progeny and companions.

The needy of Allah's forgiveness
Yahya b. al-Shaykh Muhammad b. Abi Bakr al-Mulla
May Allah pardon him

Imām Abū Bakr ibn Moḥammed al-Mullā al-Aḥsā'ī

The venerable Imam Abū Bakr ibn Moḥammed al-Mullā al-Aḥsā'ī (may Allah have mercy upon his soul) was born in the blessed city of al-Aḥsā' which is situated in eastern Ḥijāz on the second of Rabī al-Thānī in the year 1198 AH / 1784 CE.

He was orphaned while young and his upbringing fell upon the watchful eye of his mother who instilled within him a presence of the mighty and fear of his Lord. It was perceptive that a divine protection enveloped him while he continued his studies attaining mastery in many ancillary sciences, memorising the Quran while still ten years of age.

He thereafter exerted himself in attaining the sacred sciences after the age of legal discernment seeking both the revealed sacred sciences and the rational sacred sciences from the towering scholars of the region of al-Aḥsā'ī , a centre of learning and scholarship. This was in addition to studying with visiting scholars during the periods of the pilgrimage.

A person of extreme intelligence and a Godly presence who was loved by the laity and nobility. Who was of a soft nature and diplomatic when admonishing being careful not to fester hatred. Giving preference to others over himself and had a dislike for matters which caused dissension. A scrupulous aesthetic who only consumed that which was the produce of land of that which he personally owned or from endowments for which he was a rightful benefactor. His daily routine commenced during the depths of the night when the night vigil prayer was established followed by supplications for the nation of the Prophet (upon whom be peace). Following the dawn prayer a regular lesson would be delivered continuing to sunrise following which the sunrise prayer would be offered. Regular lesson would commence after each prayer and collective worship between the evening twilight and night prayer. The prayer of guidance would also be offered daily.

He was prolific in authoring many works in the various sacred disciplines which included a commentary upon al-Ṣaḥīḥ al-Bukhārī titled Irshād al-Qārī' li Ṣaḥīḥ al-Bukhārī, a commentary on Imam al-Tirmidhī's beatific attributes of the Prophet (upon whom be peace) titled Hidāyat al-Muhtazhi sharḥ Shamāil al-Tirmidhī and various texts on Hanafi jurisprudence and creed.

The Imam performed the Hajj in the year 1270AH / 1853CE following which he was overtaken by an illness and he remained in the districts of the sacred precinct. The illness took a turn for the worst and he joined the celestial realm during the 29th night of Safar. He was buried in a district of Mecca which was noted as being an abode of retirement of scholars and the pious. May Allah have mercy on his soul.

Mohammed Zaqir

After graduating from Manchester University with a BA (Hons) in Politics and Economics, Mohammed Zaqir studied in Damascus, Syria for 8 years at the Prestigious Abū Nūr Institute and studied several classical disciplines of Islamic knowledge at the hands of some of the most prominent holders of the tradition both institutionally and privately.

He has also been blessed with the opportunity to spend time in the illuminated city of Tarīm, Ḥaḍramaut; where he studied at the eminent Institute Dār al-Muṣṭafā, under the qualified hands of some of the most illustrious guides of knowledge. Being classically trained in the sacred sciences he has attained formal ijazahs in various Islamic Disciplines.

He had the honour of studying with Shaykh Adīb Kallās, Shaykh Tawfīq al-Būṭī, Shaykh Muḥammed Khayr al-Haykal, Shaykh Ḥabīb Umar bin Hafīẓ, Shaykh Ḥassān al-Hindī, Shaykh Abd al-Salām Shannār, Shaykh Sāmir al-Naṣṣ, Shaykh Abd al-Raḥmān Arjan al-Baynhwi, Shaykh Abd al-Hakim Ḥassan, Shaykh Abū Aḥmed al-Miṣrī al-Ḥanbalī, Shaykh Abd al-Qādir al-Khaṭīb, Shaykh Yāsīn Hafiẓ, Shaykh Khālid Kharṣā', Shaykh Badī' al-Sayyid al-Laḥḥām, Shaykh Iqbāl Aḥmed al-Aẓamī, Shaykh Moa'taz al-Subaynī, Shaykh Hodja Ala' al-Dīn al-Kurdī, Shaykh Moḥammed al-Jumma, Shaykh al-Mujāhid Riyāḍ al-Kirākhī and others, may Allah have mercy on them all.

Some of the texts which he studied and gained licenses to teach include Marāqī al-Falāḥ, al-Hidāyah, al-Ikhtiyār, Īḍāḥ al-Mubham Sharḥ alā al-Sulam, al-Bāqqalānis al-Insāf, al-Muwāqif, Sharḥ ala al-Aqā'id al-Nasafiyyah, Ḥashiyah alā al-Jawhara al-Tawḥīd, al-Aqīdah al-Ṭaḥāwiyyah, al-Iqtiṣād fī al-I'tiqād, Nūr al-Anwār, al-Waraqāt, Qaṭr al-Nidā, Sharḥ Ibn Aqīl alā al-Alfiyyah, Dalā'il al-Ijāz, Asrār al-Balāgah, Tafsīr al-Bayḍāwī, al-Nasafī, Nuzhat al-Naẓar, Irshād Ṭullāb al-Ḥaqā'iq and many others.

He is the director of the Darul Arqam Educational Trust in Leicester where he teaches in various venues around the country and is the Jummah lecturer during the Friday prayers and delivers weekly classes in the same institute.

Introduction

In the name of Allāh, the most Beneficent, the most Merciful

All praise is due to Allāh, and salutations and blessings upon our master, the Messenger of Allāh

To proceed: This is a compendium of *fiqh* according to the school of the great Imām, Abū Ḥanīfah (may Allāh, the Exalted, have mercy upon him) which the legally responsible person cannot forgo if unable to study that which is more detailed. I have summarised it from the books of our scholars when I realised the necessity for such a brief text, I have named it 'The Gift for the Seeker' (*Itḥāf al-Ṭālib*). I ask Allāh, glorified be He, to benefit by it all who desire to seek knowledge and teach it.

Section One

DIVINITY

Introduction

The Correct Belief: It is to know that Allāh is:

i. Existent and is necessarily existent
ii. Pre-Eternal
iii. Everlasting
iv. A Singularity
v. Self-sufficient
vi. Dissimilar to the creation

From His attributes are:

i. Life
ii. Knowledge
iii. Omnipotence
iv. Will
v. Hearing

vi. Seeing

vii. Speech

His essence does not resemble other essences and His attributes do not resemble other attributes.

He is free from attributes of deficiency.

Nothing is incumbent upon Him.

Predestination (*Qadr*), whether good or evil, is from Him.

Prophecy

He, the Exalted, sent His messengers and revealed books to them and divinely protected them from sin.

Creedal Principles

The angels are servants of Allāh and are not characterised by sin.

The miracles of the saints (*awliyā'*) are true.

Death is according to life span.

Committing major sins does not negate ones faith.

Section Two

PURIFICATION

Ablution (wuḍū')

The Compulsory Acts (*Farḍ*) of ablution (*wuḍū'*) are four:

i. Washing the face;
ii. Washing the hands including the elbows;
iii. Wiping a quarter of the head;
iv. Washing the feet, including the ankles

Its *Sunnah* acts are:

i. The intention
ii. Reciting the *basmalah*
iii. Washing the hands up to the wrists three times
iv. The toothstick
v. Washing the mouth
vi. Rinsing the nose
vii. Combing the beard

viii. Washing three times
ix. Wiping the entire head and ears
x. Order
xi. Continuity
xii. Rubbing

Its praiseworthy acts (*mustaḥabb*):

i. Beginning from the right;
ii. Wiping the neck;
iii. Reciting the transmitted invocations during it

The disliked acts (*makrūh tanzīh*) of *wuḍū'*:

i. Excessive use of water
ii. Being unduly stringent in the use of water
iii. Speech during *wuḍū's* performance
iv. Striking the water on ones face
v. Wiping one's head thrice with new water

It is nullified by:

i. That which exits from the two bodily exits
ii. The flowing of filth from other than the exits mentioned above
iii. Vomiting a mouthful but not a mouthful of phlegm
iv. Sleep of one not firmly seated
v. Unconsciousness
vi. Insanity

vii. Intoxication

viii. Audible laughter of an adult praying

ix. Obscene naked lustful embrace

Purifying bath (ghusl)

The Compulsory Acts (*farḍ*) of *ghusl*:

i. Washing the mouth;

ii. Washing the nose;

iii. Washing the entire body (It is sufficient to wet the roots of the braids of a woman)

Sunnahs of *Ghusl*:

i. To wash the hands first;

ii. Then the private parts of the body;

iii. Then to perform *wuḍū'*;

iv. To pour water over the body thrice

Ghusl is Necessitated by:

i. Ejaculation of semen accompanied by desire

ii. Inserting the head of the private part in the front or rear passages *Ghusl* is necessary upon both parties

iii. The one awakening to find semen or pre seminal fluid

iv. The end of menstruation

v. Post-natal bleeding

Ghusl is *Sunnah* for:

- i. The Friday prayer
- ii. The two *Eid* prayers
- iii. Iḥrām
- iv. ʿArafah

Water that is valid for purification

It is valid to purify with pure water, such as water from the sky and the ground, even if it changes due to remaining stagnant.

It is not permitted to use water whose qualities have been changed:

- i. Through cooking
- ii. Through being mixed with a pure substance which dominates over the attributes of the water
- iii. Due to an impurity entering it
- iv. A small amount of stagnant water in which filth has fallen
- v. Water used to remove legal impurity or water that has been used to make ablution for the purpose of drawing closer to Allāh.

Flowing or still water that reaches ten by ten cubits (5m x 5m) does not become filthy except by a trace (*athar*) becoming apparent. A trace is considered to be the presence of the taste, colour or odour of a foreign solid or liquid. This is regardless of whether the solid or liquid in question is pure or impure.

Rulings relating to remnant water

The remnants of humans are pure.

The remnants of animals whose meat it is permissible to consume are pure.

The remnants of dogs, pigs and predatory animals are filthy.

The remnants of cats, undomesticated chickens and predatory birds are disliked.

The remnants of donkeys and mules are doubtful.

Secretions of the above mentioned are given the same legal ruling as the remnants of water.

Dry ritual purification (tayammum)

One who is unable to use water due to the following reasons performs *Tayammum* :

i. The water being located beyond a mile
ii. An illness
iii. Cold
iv. Fear of an enemy
v. Thirst
vi. Absence of the means to extract the water

It is performed by:

i. Intending;
ii. Two strikes to envelope the face and hands along with the elbows

Dry ritual purification (Tayammum) is performed even if a person is in a state of major ritual impurity (*janābah*) or following the cessation of menstrual blood. *Tayammum* is performed upon a pure substance from the earth. It is valid before the time and for more than one compulsory prayer.

It is nullified by:

i. That which nullifies *wuḍū'*

ii. The ability to use water

If a greater part of one's body or body parts are injured *Tayammum* is performed; otherwise the person performs ablution and does not combine between them.

Wiping upon foot-gear or bandages

It is permissible for the one in ritual impurity (*ḥadath*) so long as it is worn whilst in a state of purity.

The time period for the resident is a day and a night, and for the traveller three days and nights, beginning when the state of purity is nullified (*ḥadath*).

Wiping is with three fingers on the upper part of the leather socks, once.

A large tear prevents it.

Wiping is nullified by:

i. That which nullifies *wuḍū'*

ii. Removing the sock

iii. The duration expires

Wiping on a bandage is akin to washing even if the bandage was tied without *wuḍū'*.

If the bandage is undone due to recuperation of one's health then wiping becomes invalid.

Menstruation

It is for a minimum of three days and a maximum of ten. Bleeding above the maximum period or less than the minimum period is considered irregular vaginal bleeding (*istiḥāḍah*). Likewise the blood which becomes apparent during pregnancy is irregular vaginal bleeding. The maximum period for post-natal bleeding (*nifās*) is forty days, there is no minimum.

The minimum purity between 'two bloods' is fifteen days.

Menstruation and post-natal bleeding make the following prohibited (*ḥarām*):

i. Prayer
ii. Fasting
iii. Recitation of the *Qur'ān* and touching it without a detachable cover
iv. Entering a mosque
v. Circumambulation of the *Ka'bah* (*ṭawāf*)
vi. A man touching his spouse in the area which is below the waist cloth

Prohibited acts whilst in a state of impurity

Major ritual impurity (*janābah*) prohibits:

i. Prayer
ii. Recitation of the *Qur'ān* and touching it
iii. Entering a mosque
iv. Circumambulation of the *Ka'bah*

It is forbidden for one in a state of minor ritual impurity (*ḥadath*) to:

i. Offer prayer

ii. Circumambulate the *Ka'bah*

iii. Touch the *Qur'ān*

One with IVB (irregular vaginal bleeding) or an excuse such as dripping of urine or a continuous nosebleed performs wuḍū' for the time of every prayer, and can offer any additional prayer alongside the compulsory prayer.

Impurities

The body and garments are cleaned with water, and with all purifying liquids.

Foot gear is purified from a solid by rubbing; a sword and its like by wiping.

The ground is purified by drying and by the disappearance of traces of the impurity.

The size of a dirham is excused from the greater impurities, such as blood, alcohol, urine of that which is not eaten and dung.

Lesser impurities are excused to the extent of that which is less than a quarter of a garment. Examples of lesser impurities include urine of animals whose meat is consumed.

That which is soiled by visible filth is purified by its removal.

Non-visible filth is purified by washing it three times.

The hide of a carcass is purified by tanning and Islamic slaughter, with the exception of the skin of pigs and humans.

The hair of humans and a carcass and their bones are pure.

Cleaning the urinary tract (istinjā')

Istinjā' is sunnah with the use of a cleansing stone, although washing is superior.

It is disliked with a bone, dung, food and with the right hand.

Facing or turning ones back to the qiblah in the bathroom; speaking; facing the sun and the moon are disliked.

Also, facing the direction of the wind and below a fruit bearing tree is disliked.

Section Three

PRAYER

The time for *Fajr* is from the true dawn until the rising of the sun. *Times of the prayer*

Ẓuhr is from the *zawāl* (zenith) until the shadow reaches twice its length in addition to the shadow (at *zawāl*).

Aṣr is from when the shade is twice its length until the setting (of the sun).

Maghrib is from sunset till the disappearance of the twilight.

Ishā and *Witr* are from the disappearance of twilight until dawn.

Its conditions are: *Conditions of the prayer*

i. Cleanliness of the body from ritual impurity and filth. One unable to find appropriate means to remove filth prays with it and there is no repetition

ii. Cleanliness of the clothing and place

iii. Covering of nakedness; a man's nakedness is from

below the navel to the knees. For a woman it is all of her body except her face, hands and feet

iv. Facing the *qiblah*. One who is unsure of the *qiblah* estimates; if they are mistaken they do not repeat the prayer

v. The time

vi. Intention

vii. Prohibiting Proclamation (*takbīr*)

Compulsory acts of prayer (Farḍ)

Its compulsory elements are:

i. Standing for one able to in other than the optional prayers

ii. Recitation of a verse in two units of the compulsory prayer and in all of the *nafl* and *witr*

iii. Bowing

iv. Prostrating

v. Performing the elements in order: standing before bowing, bowing before prostrating

vi. In the last unit, sitting for the length of the *tashahhud*

Imperative elements of prayer (wājib)

Its imperative elements (*wājib*) are:

i. Recitation of the Fātiḥah

ii. Adding a chapter or similar to the first two units of the compulsory prayers, and to all units of the *witr* and optional prayers

iii. Specifying recitation of portions of the *Qur'ān* in the first two units

iv. Order in that which is repeated in every unit

v. Tranquillity in the compulsory (*farḍ*) elements of prayer

vi. The first sitting

vii. Reciting *tashahhud* in the two sittings

viii. Pronouncing *salām* twice at the prayer's end

ix. The *qunūt* of *witr*

x. The *takbīrs* of the two Eid prayers

xi. The Imam loudly reciting in that which should be recited loudly, and silently in that which should be recited silently

Emphasised sunnah acts of prayer (sunnah mu'akadah)

The emphasised sunnah acts (*sunnah mu'akadah*) of the prayer are:

i. The *Adhān* (call to prayer)

ii. Establishing call (*iqāmah*) for the compulsory prayer

iii. Raising the hands for the prohibiting proclamation (*takbīr*)

iv. The Imam reciting the proclamations (*takbīrs*) loudly

v. The opening supplication (*thanā*)

vi. Seeking refuge (*tawudh*)

vii. Saying Bismillah (*tasmiyah*)

viii. Saying Amin

ix. Placing the right hand over the left below the navel

x. That the *sūrah* be from the *ṭiwāl al-mufaṣṣal* in the Fajr and Ẓuhr prayers, from the *Awsaṭ* in the Aṣr and Ishā prayers, and from the *qiṣār* in the Maghrib prayer

xi. Proclamation (*takbīr*) of bowing (*ruku*) and its praises (*tasbīḥ*) thrice

xii. Grasping the knees with the hands

xiii. Spreading the fingers and straightening ones back

xiv. Rising from bowing (*rukū*)

xv. The Imam uttering the *tasmī'*, and the follower uttering the *taḥmīd* The one praying alone combines between both

xvi. Placing the knees then the hands then the face for prostration, and its reverse when rising

xvii. *Takbīr* for prostration and rising from it, saying its *tasbīḥ* thrice

xviii. A man separating the elbows from the sides, and the stomach from the thighs. Separating the arms from the ground is necessary for both men and women

xix. Sitting placing the hands between prostrations on the thighs as one would do in the *tashahhud* posture

xx. Spreading out the left foot, raising the right during the sitting postures

xxi. Reciting the Fatihah in other than the first two units of the compulsory prayer

xxii. Salutations upon the Prophet (Allāh bless him and grant him peace) in the final sitting

xxiii. Supplicating with the transmitted Quranic or prophetic prayers

xxiv. Turning whilst pronouncing the two *salāms*

Desirable sunnah acts of prayer (ādab)

The desirable sunnah acts of prayer are:

i. Looking to the place of prostration whilst standing
ii. Looking to the upper part of the feet when bowing
iii. Looking to the nose when prostrating
iv. Looking to the lap when sitting
v. Bringing out the hands from the sleeves at the time of *takbīr*
vi. Covering the mouth when yawning
vii. *Tartīl* of recitation
viii. A distance of four fingers between the feet when standing
ix. Pointing with the index finger during tashahhud when bearing witness
x. Standing when *'Ḥayy ala al-Ṣalah'* is said

The nullifiers of prayer

Prayer is nullified by:

i. Speech
ii. Supplicating with that which resembles speech
iii. Offering the greeting of *Saām* and replying to it
iv. Excessive movement
v. Turning the chest away from the direction of the *qiblah*
vi. Eating
vii. Drinking
viii. Coughing without an excuse

ix. Groaning (*al-inin*)

x. Moaning (*tawwuh*)

xi. Replying to someone who has sneezed

xii. Replying to speech even with *Dhikr*

xiii. Prompting/correcting an Imam of prayer other than his own

xiv. Reciting from a copy of the Quran (*mushaf)*

Disliked actions

The disliked (*makrūh*) acts of prayer are:

i. Fiddling with clothing and body

ii. Placing hands on the hips

iii. Turning around

iv. Spreading out the arms

v. Squatting

vi. Placing the arms on the ground

vii. Rolling up the sleeves

viii. Replying to *salām* with a gesture

ix. Tying up the hair

x. Uncovering the head

xi. Hanging clothing

xii. Praying in unkempt clothes

xiii. Starting the prayer whilst repressing the urge to relieve oneself

xiv. Yawning if one is able to repress it

xv. Closing the eyes or raising them to the sky

xvi. Wiping dust from the forehead

xvii. Wearing a garment containing an image of a living being

xviii. That an image of a living being which posseses a soul be above the head or in front of one offering prayer

xix. Counting verses and *tasbīḥ* with the hand

xx. Placing something in the mouth which prevents the *sunnah* recitation

xxi. Supporting/leaning against a wall and its like without excuse

xxii. Praying towards the face of another or towards fire

xxiii. Praying on the road

xxiv. Praying in a bathroom or graveyard, or praying on another's land without their consent

xxv. With the presence of food that a person desires, or with the presence of filth which does not prevent the prayer

xxvi. Reciting in other than the standing posture

xxvii. Lengthening the second unit over the first

xxviii. Repeating a chapter in all units of the compulsory prayer

xxix. Reciting a chapter previous than the one recited in a unit or two units

xxx. Smelling fragrance

xxxi. Turning the fingers from the *qiblah*

xxxii. Non-excessive movement

xxxiii. Covering the nose and mouth

xxxiv. Prostrating on the coil of the turban

xxxv. Limiting it to the forehead and excluding the nose without a valid excuse

The uneven (Witr) and optional prayers (Nafl)

The *witr* is imperative. It is three units with one salām. The Fatihah and a surah are recited in all units. The Submission Prayer (*duā al-Qunūt*) is performed in the third before bowing. It is not performed in other than the third unit. Witr is offered in congregation in Ramaḍān only.

The emphasised and desirable sunnah units of prayer (sunnan mu'akadah)

The emphasised *Sunnah* are :

i. Two units before *Fajr*

ii. Two units after *Ẓuhr, Maghrib* and *Ishā*

iii. Four before *Ẓuhr* and *Jum'ah*, and after it

The desirable *Sunnah* are :

i. Four before *Aṣr*

ii. Four before *Ishā* and after it

iii. Four after *Ẓuhr*

iv. Six after *Maghrib*

All the four units are completed with two salāms at the end of the four units.

Rulings for the optional prayers (nafl)

Optional prayers can be offered sitting despite the ability to stand, or riding outside of the city, in which case they can be offered by gesturing to any direction that the animal [means of transport] is facing. The compulsory and imperative prayers are not offered on an animal except due to an excuse.

The night Ramaḍān vigil prayer (tarawih)

It is an emphasised *Sunnah* in *Ramaḍān* to offer twenty units after *Ishā* in congregation. It is a desirable *Sunnah* to complete the recitation of the *Quran.*

Leading the prayer

A lone person stands to the right of the Imam, two people stand behind him.

It is not valid for:

i. A man to follow a woman or a child
ii. The pure to follow one with a legally valid excuse
iii. The literate to follow the illiterate
iv. The clothed to follow the naked
v. The one praying the compulsory to follow behind someone offering an optional prayer

Following is prevented by a road or path through which a plough attached to a bull or small boat passes, or a space in the desert of two rows width, or a wall which prevents knowing the position of the Imam.

The one in wudu following the one who has performed Tayammum is valid. Likewise the one who has washed behind the one who has wiped is also valid.

The one standing behind the one seated, and the one gesturing behind the one gesturing are also considered to be valid. Also the one offering optional prayers behind the one offering compulsory prayers is likewise valid.

If it becomes apparent that the Imams prayer is invalid the follower repeats it.

Travellers' prayer

The one who leaves his place of residence intending a journey of 51 imperial miles offers the four unit compulsory (*farḍ*) prayer as two units until he returns to his place of residence or intends to reside at a place for half a month.

If the traveller completes his prayers as four and he sat in the first tashahhud sitting the prayer is valid. And if the traveller did not sit in the first tashahhud the prayer is invalid. If a traveller prays behind a resident in the time it is valid and he completes the prayer as four. The missed prayers of the journey and residency are made up as two and four units.

The prayer of the ill person

The one unable to stand due to illness, or who fears an increase in his illness if he stands, prays sitting with bowing and prostrating. If he is unable to do this then he prays with gestures whilst seated. If he is unable to sit then he prays by gestures lying down, on the back or the side. In the absence of ability to do what we have previously mentioned the prayer is delayed.

Performing missed prayers

The order between the missed and current prayers is necessary. Maintaining order is no longer necessary due to the lack of time, forgetfulness and the number of compulsory missed prayers reaching six (the imperative prayer is not to be considered).

If the compulsory is offered whilst aware of the missed prayers the compulsory prayers are invalidated.

Prostration of forgetfulness

It is imperative to prostrate twice with the tashahhud and salām if he has omitted an imperative (*wājib*) act forgetfully even if more than one imperative act was omitted.

It is incumbent on the follower due to the forgetfulness of his Imam.

The one who forgets the first sitting returns to it as long as he has not stood up fully.

If he forgets the last he returns as long as he has not prostrated, if he did prostrate the compulsory becomes optional and adds a sixth unit. If he sat for the last then stood he returns and makes *salām* if this is before he prostrates in the next unit. If however he prostrates in the next unit (the fifth unit for example) his compulsory is completed and he adds a sixth unit and prostrates for forgetfulness.

If he is inflicted by doubt he acts upon his dominant view (*ghalib ẓann*).

Prostration of recitation

It is imperative (*wājib*) for the reciter of the Quran and the listener to prostrate when a verse from the fourteen verses of the Quran which require prostration is recited. The first being in Surat 'al-Ḥajj'

It is imperative on the follower by the recitation of his Imam if he prostrates. If it is heard by the one praying from other than his Imam he prostrates after the prayer. Its Method is to prostrate with the conditions of the prayer between two takbīrs without raising.

The Friday prayer (jumah)

It is an individual compulsory act (*farḍ*). The conditions for its validity are:

i. A town/city

ii. The ruler is the Imam or his representative

iii. The time of *Ẓuhr*

iv. The sermon in the time of Ẓuhr before the Jumah prayer

v. General permission for the public

vi. The congregation – the least of which is three individuals

The conditions for it being compulsory are:

i. Residence

ii. To be of the masculine gender

iii. Freedom

iv. Sound health

Miscellaneous Issues:

One who joins the Friday prayer at the *tashahhud* completes the Friday prayer (*Jumah*) as two units.

It is imperative to perform *Jumah* and leave trading with the first call to prayer (*adhān*).

It is recommended (*sunnah*) that the *Imam* deliver two sermons sitting between them.

The Eid prayer

It is imperative upon whom the Friday prayer is imperative with its conditions except the sermon. Its time is from the rising of the sun until the zenith (*zawāl*).

Its method is to offer two units:

i. Reciting the praise (*thanā*) before the additional *takbīrs;*

ii. Perform *takbīr* for them raising the hands;

iii. Then recite the *Fatihah* and a chapter;

iv. Then bow;

v. When he stands for the second he begins with the recitation, then makes *takbīr* for the extra *takbīrs* thrice

vi. If the *takbīrs* are pronounced in the second unit before the recitation it is permissible

vii. Thereafter the Imam delivers two sermons after the prayer

The '*takbīr of tashrīq*' is imperative once after every compulsory prayer, from the Fajr of Arafah till the last of the 'days of *tashrīq*'.

The funeral prayer

It is a communal obligation similar to washing, shrouding and burying. The conditions for the validity of funeral prayer are:

i. The deceased should be a Muslim

ii. In a state of purity

The Foundational Elements (*rukn*) are:

iii. The *takbīrs*

iv. Standing

The *Sunnah* Aspects are:

i. Standing of the Imam in line with the chest of the deceased

ii. The praise (*thanā*) after the first *takbīr*

iii. Salutations upon the Prophet (Allāh bless Him and grant Him peace) after the second *takbīr*

iv. Supplication after the third *takbīr*

v. *Salām* after the fourth

If he is buried without prayer, it is offered at the grave as long as it is thought that the body has not decomposed. A new born who dies is prayed over if when born it makes a sound indicating its life prior to its death, otherwise no prayer is performed.

Section Four

POOR DUE (ZAKĀH)

Those who must pay poor due (zakāh)

Poor Due is compulsory upon (*farḍ*) for

i. The Muslim who is free
ii. The Muslim who is responsible
iii. Possessor of the minimum threshold (*al-Niṣāb*) which has the ability to increase for a full lunar year
iv. Being free from debt
v. Possessing wealth in excess of one's basic needs

[Sections of Poor Due concerning livestock and farm land shall not be translated here for lack of relevance - translator]

The minimum threshold (*al-Niṣāb*) is twenty '*mithqāl*'[1] for gold and two hundred '*dirhams*' for silver, regardless of whether the gold or silver are nuggets, jewellery or trading goods. The minimum threshold can be paid according to any one of the two amounts.

The necessary amount to pay is a quarter of a tenth [2.5%] and

1 Equivalent to 100g for gold and 700g for silver.

the value of the trading goods is added to one of the two amounts when calculating the amount to pay.

Poor Due may be paid to:

Recipients of poor due (zakāh)

i. The poor
ii. The destitute
iii. The collector of Poor Due
iv. The slave securing his freedom
v. The indebted
vi. One in the path of Allāh
vii. The traveller

It can be spent on one category or many.

Poor Due cannot be spent on:

i. Ones offspring
ii. Ones parents or their parents
iii. Ones wife or a wife spending upon her husband
iv. It cannot be given to the wealthy or his bondsman
v. Cannot be given to *Bani Hāshim* or their patrons

He who pays Poor Due to one he thinks to be eligible and it transpires other than this; the Poor Due is enacted.

To transport Poor Due is disliked except if it is to ones relatives or to one in greater need.

The one who possesses a food ration for the day does not beg.

Post Ramaḍān charity (sadaqah al-fitr)

It is imperative upon the free Muslims who possess the minimum threshold (*al Niṣāb*), or on those who possess wealth in excess of one's basic human needs and that of his poor small children or his slave whom he utilises for domestic duties.

It is not imperative upon him to pay for his wife or his older children.

The imperative amount to spend is half of a *ṣā'*[2] of wheat or a *ṣā'* of dates or barley[3]. It is paid from the dawn of Fajr of the first day of Eid al-Fitr and it is correct if it precedes this time and if it is delayed after it; it is enacted.

2 Equivalent to 1.82 kg.
3 Equivalent to 3.64 kg.

Section Five

FASTING (SAWM)

Fasting is of four types:

The types of fast

i. Compulsory fasting (*farḍ*), such as the fast of Ramaḍān

ii. Imperative fasting (*wājib*), such as for a vow[4]

iii. Optional fasting (*sunnah*), for a reason other than the previous two

iv. Gravely disliked fasting (*makrūh taḥrīmī*), such as on the two *Eids* or the days of *tashriq*

That for which it is not necessary to specify the intention:

i. The fast of the current *Ramaḍān*

---

4 The author commented on this saying: This is if it was general such as his saying: O Allāh such and such a fast is (incumbent) upon me, or suspended with a condition that he wishes to occur such as his saying: If Allāh cures my illness then such and such a fast is (incumbent) upon me. As for if he suspends it with a condition that he does not wish to occur such as his saying: If I speak to Zayd then such and such (is incumbent) upon me. He has a choice between fulfilling it or an making an expiation for an oath.

ii. The fast for a specific vow

Optional fasting is valid with an intention from the night up till before midday and with a general intention.

It is a condition for the remaining types of fasts that it be from the night [ie. before dawn] and it be specified

Sighting the new moon

The one who sights the new moon for the commencement of *Ramaḍān* or the new moon for the completion of *Ramaḍān* and the Islamic judge (*Qāḍī)* rejects his testimony fasts individually.

That which invalidates the fast

The fast is not invalidated[5] by:

i. Eating, drinking, or engaging in marital relations forgetfully

ii. A wet dream

iii. Ejaculating due to looking

iv. Applying oil or antimony

v. Cupping

vi. Kissing

vii. Swallowing dust or a flea enters one's throat

viii. Oil being poured in the urinary tract

ix. Water in the ear

x. Tasting something with the mouth

xi. Overcoming vomiting and it returns accidentally

5 In Arabic the term *fāsid* has been used, which in acts of worship is the same as the term batil. In other chapters of fiqh other than worship fasid and batil are not identical. See Ḥāshiyah al-Ṭaḥṭāwi alā Marāqī al-Falāḥ (p.397).

The following invalidates the fast without expiation:

i. Breaking the fast accidentally then continuing eating or cohabiting

ii. Applying medication via the rear passageway or via the nose

iii. Dripping oil in to the ear

iv. Swallowing a stone

v. Fasting without making intention (in *Ramaḍān*)

vi. Rain entering the throat

vii. Ejaculation which is self induced or due to kissing

viii. Invalidates other than the Ramaḍān fast

ix. Having a pre-dawn meal thinking that it is not yet dawn

In these circumstances, one makes up the invalidated fast only.

Upon whom it is imperative (*wājib*) to refrain from eating during the day of *Ramaḍān*:

i. One whose fast has been invalidated

ii. Likewise a traveller who [becomes a] resident

iii. A menstruating woman who purifies

iv. A child who reached maturity

v. A disbeliever who embraces Islam

That which invalidates the fast and expiation is necessary along with a 'makeup fast' (*Qaḍā*):

i. It is invalidated if one has marital relations in any of the two private openings deliberately

ii. If one eats, or drinks food[6] deliberately

iii. If one consumes medication deliberately

In this case, the individual makes up and expiates like the expiation of *al-Ẓihār*[7].

The following is disliked for the fasting person, but does not break the fast:

i. To taste something or chew gum

ii. Kissing and physical contact if one is not sure about the possibility of this leading on to intercourse

It is desirable to take a pre dawn meal, delaying it, and hastening to open the fast

6 The basis for this is that which is reported by the six Imams and others that the Prophet (Allāh bless Him and give Him peace) ordered a person who had marital relations deliberately during the day in *Ramaḍān* to offer the expiation like that of *al-Ẓihār* as mentioned in *Surah al-Mujādilah*. The scenario of eating and drinking deliberately taking the same ruling of expiation is because they are equivalent in deliberately invalidating the fast and the obtaining of pleasure and fulfilling desire. As for that which is reported by *al-Dārquṭnī* from *Abū Mashar*, from *Muḥammad bin Kab al-Qurzi*, from *Abū Hurayrah* that a man ate in *Ramaḍān*, and the Prophet (Allāh bless Him and give Him peace) ordered him to free a slave or to fast two months, or feed 60 poor people. Except that it has been weakened by the presence of the narrator *Abū Mashar*. See *Fatḥ Bāb al-Ināyah* (1/568).

7 In the *shariah* '*al-Ẓihār*' is defined as a man saying to his wife :'You are to me like the back of my mother'. See *Anees al-Fuqaha* p.162. By a man saying this it is unlawful for him to have martial relations and that which precedes it such as touching and kissing with his wife until he gives expiation (*kaffārah*) for his '*Ẓihār*'. This is due to His (the Exalted) words: And those who make unlawful to them (their wives) (by al-*Ẓihār*) and wish to free themselves from what they uttered, (the penalty) in that case (is) the freeing of a slave before they touch each other. That is an admonition to you (so that you may not return to such an ill thing). And Allāh is All-Aware of what you do. And he who finds not (the money for freeing a slave) must fast two successive months before they both touch each other. And for him who is unable to do so, he should feed sixty of *Miskīn* (poor). That is in order that you may have perfect Faith in Allāh and His Messenger. These are the limits set by Allāh. And for disbelievers, there is a painful torment. See *Sharḥ al-Kanz of al-Aini* (2/169)

The reasons permitting one not to fast

Abstaining from the fast is permitted for:

i. The traveller

ii. A pregnant woman

iii. A suckling woman if she fears for herself or her child

iv. An ill person who fears an increase may similarly not fast

And they make up a missed fast at their earliest convenience.

The above mentioned are not required to fast although a makeup fast is necessary.

A terminally old person does not fast and gives *fidya*.

An optional fast is necessary to make-up once started and then invalidated. An optional fast is not invalidated without reason.

Spiritual seclusion (i'tikaf)

It is to reside within a congregational mosque coupled with an intention. It is imperative to perform the spiritual seclusion if one has a taken a vow, and it is an emphasised *sunnah* in the last ten days of *Ramaḍān*. It is desirable in other than the last ten days. A person who has taken a vow for spiritual seclusion then fasting together with it is also necessary.

The least amount for the optional period of *Itikāf* is a moment.

One does not leave from the place of *Itikāf* except for answering human needs and the Friday prayer. He eats, drinks and sleeps in the *masjid*.

Itikāf is invalidated by marital relations and ejaculation.

Vowing Itikāf during the days consecutively necessarily also renders the nights necessary.

Section Six

PILGRIMAGES (HAJJ & ʿUMRAH)

Compulsory elements of the pilgrimage

The major pilgrimage (*Ḥajj*) is compulsory (*farḍ*) once upon the person who is:

i. Muslim

ii. Free

iii. Adult

iv. Healthy

v. Possessing provision and transport in excess of basic necessities

vi. Sure of the safety of the route

Its compulsory (*farḍ*) elements are:

i. *Iḥrām*

ii. Standing in Arafah

iii. *Ṭawāf al-Ziyārah*

Its imperative (*wājib*) elements are:

i. *Iḥrām* from the *Mīqāt*

ii. Lengthening of the stay/standing till sunset

iii. Standing in *Muzdalifah*

iv. Stoning the three pillars

v. Shaving or trimming of the hair

vi. Performing the *Ṭawāf al-Ifāḍah* during the days of *al-naḥr*

vii. *Saiee* walking

viii. *Ṭawāf al-Widā*, starting the *Ṭawāf* from the black stone, walking with purity during it and covering ones nakedness

Its Months are:

i. *Shawwāl,*

ii. *Dhu al-Qadah*

iii. 10 days of *Dhu al-Ḥijjah*

Iḥrām for Hajj is disliked before it.

The Rulings for Umrah:

i. *Iḥrām*

ii. *Ṭawāf*

iii. *Saiee*

The Umrah is sunnah. It is disliked on the day of Arafah and the four days after it (days of Tashrīq).

A description of the performance of the acts of Hajj in the sunnah manner

The one who wishes to enter *Iḥrām* performs *wudu*, though bathing is superior. They then wear the waist wrap (*izār*) and mantle, apply fragrance and offer two units, saying: "O Allāh, I Intend Hajj so make it easy for me and accept it from me."

They then recite the talbiyah after the prayer intending Hajj, and they avoid indecent talk, sinning, arguing, killing hunted land animals, applying fragrance, covering the head and face, shaving hair, cutting nails, wearing stitched clothing and footgear (*khuffain*), and clothes coloured with dye that posses fragrance.

The *talbiyah* is recited frequently with a raised voice.

When one enters Makkah one starts with the masjid and faces the black-stone, making takbīr and tahlil. They raise the hands in greeting (*istilām*) without harming any one. They perform the Ṭawāf of Qudoom whilst exposing the right shoulder (*iḍṭibā*), with seven circuits and raml in the first three. One must greet the stone each time one passes it in each of the seven circuits, finishing the Ṭawāf with a final greeting.

Then one performs two units of prayer which are imperative (*wājib*) after every seven circuits. Thereafter one drinks the water of Zamzam and then greets (*istalām*) the black-stone. They then exit and ascend al-Safa facing the sacred-house, making takbīr, tahlil, sending Salutations upon the Prophet (Allāh bless him and give him peace), and supplicating raising the hands. They then hasten between the two indicated points. This is performed seven times, with the final circuit ending at al-Marwa.

Finally to leave the state of Iḥrām one either shaves his hair (which is preferable for men) or cut at least one fourth of his hair. Women cut and do not shave.

Section Seven

THE FORBIDDEN AND THE PERMISSIBLE

It is prohibitively disliked (*makruh tahrim*):

i. To consume the flesh of a female donkey and it's milk.

ii. To eat, drink or apply perfume from a gold or a sliver vessel by men or women.

iii. It is permissible to drink from a vessel decorated or plated by silver but the places where there is silver should be avoided when drinking from it.

iv. It is prohibited to wear silk for men not for women. Men may wear silk only the area of four fingers [like an emblem]. It is permissible for clothing of different materials to be sown by silk or for silk lines running down a garment or across it.

v. It is impermissible for the man to wear jewellery of gold or silver except a silver ring, a girdle belt decorated with silver or a decorative handle of the sword. Wearing a ring should be of silver only and not of any other substance.

vi. It is prohibitively disliked to dress a male child in silk or gold

Section Eight

REGARDING MISCELLANEOUS ISSUES

The vomit of a mouse does not spoil butter, clarified butter or water except if the taste or colour of the vomit becomes apparent.

The head of a sheep which is permeated by blood and it is burnt till all the blood disappears and then it is used to produce a gravy or soup, is permissible.

If an intention is made for a *Qadha* fast (make up) for *Ramadhan* and a particular day is not specified it is correct.

It is prohibitively disliked (*makruh tahrim*) to consume from a sheep its vulva and surrounding areas, testicles, scrotum, parathyroid gland, ganglion lump ,bladder, gall bladder , flowing blood and the penis.

Racing with a one sided wager [ie if this horse wins for eg. I will give an amount] with horses, camels, on foot and archery are permissible. As for any competition where there is no wager it is permissible. A two sided wager from either slide is impermissible.

A one sided wager is permissible - whereby one states to the other if your horse wins the race I will surrender a sum to you and if your horse wins you do not surrender any amount to me.

CLOTHING

It is praiseworthy to wear black and to wear a turban in which the tail of the turban is hanging/flowing between the shoulders [to the middle of his back].

It is disliked to wear clothing which is yellow or saffron

It is permissible to beautify the Quranic Scripture.

It is permissible for a non Muslim subject (*dhimmi*) to enter a mosque and to visit a sick non Muslim

It is permissible to castrate an animal

Playing Backgammon is prohibitively disliked

Hoarding the staple diet of people and animals is prohibitively disliked

The Epilogue

CONCERNING INTERNAL PURIFICATION

It is divesting the heart from all besides Allāh the most high and to disdain other than Him. And to be aware of Allāh in all your affairs, such that if you begin performing an imperative act, or leave a forbidden act and thereafter begin an optional or an undesirable act, it is with the awareness of Allāh.

One should be anxious to leave the prohibited, and this concern should be more intense than performing the commanded obligations and to believe that what you have performed is deficient and that you have failed to fulfil what is incumbent upon you by Allāh to the equivalent of an iota. And that you are not better than another Muslim for indeed you are not aware what will be your ending nor what will be another's ending. And surrender the matter to the command and decree of Allāh being convinced that what will occur will not be except that which he intends. And be mindful that you do not judge the conditions of people or to treat them with patronage and honour except in a situation in which the law has permitted.

And summon to your mind three principles:

Firstly, there is no benefit or harm except from Him the most high, that he has apportioned for you sustenance from pre-eternity which will reach you.

Secondly, you are indeed a fettered slave and that it is for your Lord to administer you however He wishes and that it is repugnant that you should dislike that which your master does with you - He who is more tender with you and more merciful with you than even yourself and parents. And He is the most precise in judgement regarding His actions. He does not desire that an injury should reach you except for your probity.

Thirdly, that the world is perishing and indeed the hereafter is advancing, remaining, eternal. And that you are in the world a guest and there is no doubt that your journey must conclude, and you will definitely reach your abode. So endure and tolerate the tribulations and difficulties of the journey that will end soon. And endeavour in building your abode to ameliorate it and beatify it in this short span so you can enjoy for a period of eternal continuance without end. And Allāh is the most aware.

And salutations upon our leader Muhammad (upon whom be peace) and upon his family, companions in continuance for the duration of the times he is remembered and the times for which the heedless are unmindful of him and profuse blessings be upon him in abundance.

Appendix

SELECTED PRAYERS

BEFORE WUDU

It is narrated from the Companions:

بسمِ اللهِ الْعَظِيْمِ و الْحَمْدُ للهِ على دينِ الإسْلامِ

Bismillāh al-Aẓīm Wa al-Ḥamdu Lillāhi alā' Dīn al-Islām

In the name of Allah the Mighty and all praise to Allah for revealing the religion of Islam

AFTER WUDU

To recite the prayer:

اللَّهُمّ اجْعَلْنِي مِنَ التَّوَّابِيْنَ و اجْعَلْنِي مِنَ المُتَطَهِّرِيْنَ

Allahumma Ajalnī min at-Tawābīn
wa Ajalnī min al-Mutaṭahhirīn

O Allah ! Make me from those who
are repentant and make me from the purified

THE CALL TO PRAYER (*ADHAN*)

The Adhan and the iqamah (*iqāma*)are strongly emphasised sunnahs (*sunna mu'akkada*) for compulsory prayers whether alone or in a congregation, offered in its appointed time or lapsed (*qaḍā*), for the traveller or resident. It is strongly preferred for women to offer their salat individually hence a woman offering the Adhan is disliked. The formula is :

اللّٰهُ أَكْبَرُ

Four times

أَشْهَدُ أَنْ لَا إِلَهَ إِلَّا اللّٰهُ

Twice

أَشْهَدُ أَنَّ مُحَمَّدًا رَسُولُ اللّٰهِ

Twice

حَيَّ عَلَى الصَّلَاةِ

Twice

حَيَّ عَلَى الْفَلَاحِ

Twice

اللّٰهُ أَكْبَرُ

Twice

لَا إِلَهَ إِلَّا اللّٰهُ

Once

When one recites the two statements testifying the unity of Allah one must not do so in a quavering raising tone whereby the first is said in a low voice and the second in a raised voice. This practice is known as tarje'e (*tarjī'*) and it is disliked (*makrūh*). To say the Adhan slowly and stop between each phrase that allows for a listener to reply is praiseworthy. And to repeat it from the beginning should one stop.

PRAYER ON THE COMPLETION OF ADHAN

Once the Adhan is complete one recites salutations upon the Prophet (peace be upon him) thereafter followed by the supplication :

اللَّهُمَّ رَبَّ هَذِهِ الدَّعْوَةِ التَّامَةِ والصَّلَاةِ القَايِمَةِ
آتِ سيدَنا محمداً الوسلية والفضيلة وابعثْهُ مقاماً
محموداً الذى وعدْتَهُ

Allāhumma rabba hāthihi ad-da'wah al-tāmah wa aṣ-ṣalāt al-qāimah āti sayidanā Muḥammad al-wasīlata wa'l-faḍīlata wa'b'aathhu maqāman mahmūda allathī wa'dtuhu

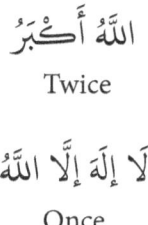

O Allah! Owner of this perfect call and owner of this established prayer bestow upon Mohammed (peace be upon him) a station of a intermediary and a station of excellence and send him to a raised praised station that you have promised him

THE OPENING SUPPLICATION (*THANĀ*)

سَبَحانَكَ اللَّهُمَّ وَبِحَمْدِكَ وَتَبَارَكَ اسْمُكَ وَتَعَالَى
جَدُّكَ وَلا إِلَهَ غَيْرُكَ

Subḥānaka Allāhumma wa bi ḥamdika wa tabāraka asmuka wa ta'ālā jadduka wa lā ilāha ghayruk

Glorified are You O Allah ! Praise belongs to You. Blessed is Your name. Exalted is Your dominion. And there is no god other than You.

THE TAWUDH

أَعُوذُ باللهِ مِنَ الشَيْطَانِ الرجيمِ

Aū'dhu bi Allāhi mina as-shayṭān ir-rajīm

I seek protection of Allah from the satan, the accursed

BOWING (*RUKU*)

سَبْحَانَ رَبِّيَ العَظِيْم

Subḥāna rabbi al-ʿaẓīm – thrice

Glory be to my lord the Great

RISING FROM BOWING (*RUKŪ*) TO THE STANDING POSITION

سَمِعَ اللهُ لِمَنْ حَمِدَه

Samiʿa Allāhu liman ḥamidah

Allah hears those that praise Him

STANDING POSITION AFTER RUKU

اللهمَّ ربَّنا و لَكَ الحَمْد

Allāhumma rabbanā wa laka al-ḥamd.

O Allah ! Our lord for You is all praise

WHILE IN PROSTRATION

سُبْحَانَ رَبِّيَ الأَعْلَى

Subḥāna rabbi al-a'alā - thrice.

Glorified be my lord the Most high

THE TASHAHHUD

التَّحِيَّاتُ لِلَّهِ وَالصَّلَوَاتُ وَالطَّيِّبَاتُ السَّلَامُ عَلَيْكَ
أَيُّهَا النَّبِيُّ وَرَحْمَةُ اللَّهِ وَبَرَكَاتُهُ السَّلَامُ عَلَيْنَا وَعَلَى
عِبَادِ اللَّهِ الصَّالِحِينَ أَشْهَدُ أَنْ لَا إِلَهَ إِلَّا اللَّهُ وَأَشْهَدُ
أَنَّ مُحَمَّدًا عَبْدُهُ وَرَسُولُهُ

Attaḥiyyātu lillāhi waṣ-ṣalawātu waṭṭayibātu as-salām alayka ayyuhan an-nabiyyu wa raḥmatullāhi wa barakātuh. Assalāmu alaynā wa alā ibadāAllah aṣ-ṣālihī. Ashadu ala ilahāh illal Allāh wa ashadu anna Moḥammadan a'bduhū wa rasūluh

All perfect greetings, prayers and goodness are for Allah. Salutations upon you O Prophet and Allah's mercy and blessings. Salutations also be upon us and upon the pious servants of Allah. I testify that there is no god except Allah and I bear witness that Mohammed is His servant and messenger.

SALUTATIONS UPON THE PROPHET ﷺ

اللَّهُمَّ صَلِّ عَلَى مُحَمَّدٍ وَعَلَى آلِ مُحَمَّدٍ كَمَا صَلَّيْتَ
عَلَى إِبْرَاهِيمَ وَعَلَى آلِ إِبْرَاهِيمَ وَبَارِكْ عَلَى مُحَمَّدٍ وَعَلَى
آلِ مُحَمَّدٍ كَمَا بَارَكْتَ عَلَى إِبْرَاهِيمَ وَعَلَى آلِ إِبْرَاهِيمَ
فِي الْعَالَمِينَ إِنَّكَ حَمِيدٌ مَجِيدٌ

Allāhumma Ṣalli 'alā Muḥammadin wa 'alā āli Muḥammadin kamā Ṣallayta 'alā Ibrāhīma wa 'alā āli Ibrāhīma wa Bārik 'alā Muḥammadin wa 'alā āli Muḥammadin kamā Bārakta 'alā Ibrāhīma wa 'alā āli Ibrāhīma fi al-Ālamīn innaka Ḥamīdum Majīd.

O Allah ! Grant mercy to Mohammed and to the family of Mohammed as You have granted mercy to Ibrahim and the family of Ibrahim and bless Mohammed and the family of Mohammed just as you have blessed Ibrahim and on the family of Ibrahim, throughout the world. Verily you are the most praiseworthy and glorious.

SALAMS

السَّلَامُ عَلَيْكُمْ وَرَحْمَةُ اللَّه

'Assalām Alaykum Waraḥmatullāh'

The peace and mercy of Allah be upon you

THE QUNUT PRAYER (HUMILITY AND SUBMISSION PRAYER)

اللَّهُمَّ إنَّا نَسْتَعِيْنَكَ ونَسْتَهْدِيْكَ ونَسْتَغْفِرُكَ ونَتُوْبُ
إلَيْكَ ونُؤْمِنُ بِكَ ونَتَوَكَّلُ عَلَيْكَ ونَثْنِي عَلَيْكَ
الخَيْرَ كُلَّهُ نَشْكُرُكَ ولا نَكْفُرُكَ ونَخْلَعُ ونَتْرُكُ مَنْ
يَفْجُرُكَ اللَّهُمَّ إيَّاكَ نَعْبُدُ ولَكَ نُصَلِّ ونَسْجُدُ وإلَيْكَ
نَسْعَى ونَحْفِدُ نَرْجُو رَحْمَتَكَ ونَخْشَى عَذَابَكَ إنَّ
عَذَابَكَ الجِدَّ بالكُفَّارِ مُلْحَقٌ وصَلَّى الله على سَيِّدِنا
النَبِيّ وآلِهِ وسَلَّمَ

Allāhumma Inna nasta'īnaka wa nastahdīka wa nastaghfiruka wa natūbu Ilayka wa nu'minu bika wa natawakkulu alayka wa nathnī alayka al-khayr kulluhu nashkuruka wa la nakfuruka wa nakhla'u wa natruku man yafjuruka. Allāhumma iyyāka na'budu wa laka nuṣallī wa nasjudu wa ilayka nas'ā wa nahfidu wa narjū raḥmataka wa nakhshā adhābaka inna adhābaka al-jidda bil-kuffāri mulḥiq wa ṣalla Allāhu alā an-nabiyyi wa ālihi wa sallam.

O Allah ! We seek your help and beg of your forgiveness and affirm our faith in You and rely on You and praise You and thank You and we do not withhold our gratitude from you and we cast off and leave one who disobeys You. O Allah! You alone do we worship and to You we offer prayer and prostrate before you and traverse and rush towards you and hope for Your mercy, and dread your punishment. Indeed your punishment will over come the disbelievers.

If one does not know the prayer one can say any Quranic or Prophetic prayer.

www.ingramcontent.com/pod-product-compliance
Lightning Source LLC
Chambersburg PA
CBHW031232120626
46545CB00003B/1099
* 9 7 8 1 9 9 9 8 5 7 4 5 5 *